What's Inside?

Submarines

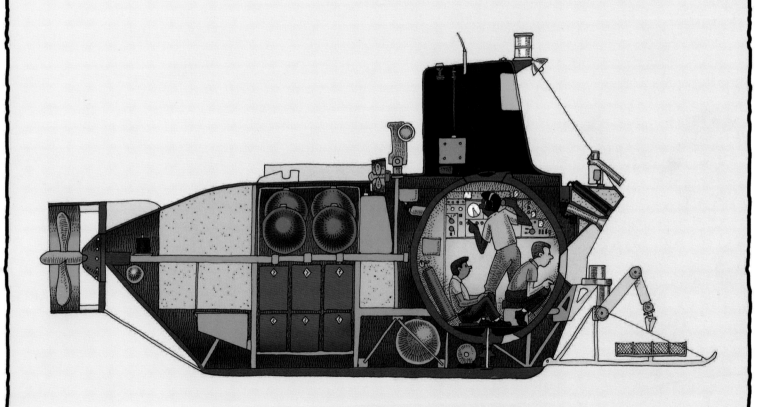

A+

Smart Apple Media

Published by Smart Apple Media, an imprint of Black Rabbit Books
P.O. Box 3263, Mankato, Minnesota 56002
www.blackrabbitbooks.com

Produced by David West 🏃 Children's Books
6 Princeton Court, 55 Felsham Road, London SW15 1AZ

Designed and illustrated by David West

Cataloging-in-Publication data is on file with the Library of Congress.
ISBN 978-1-62588-405-3
eBook ISBN 978-1-62588-434-3

Printed in China
CPSIA compliance information: DWCB16CP
010116

9 8 7 6 5 4 3 2 1

Contents

The First Submarines

The first submarine was made in 1620. Soon, they were used in wars.

Bushnell's Turtle

Breathing tube

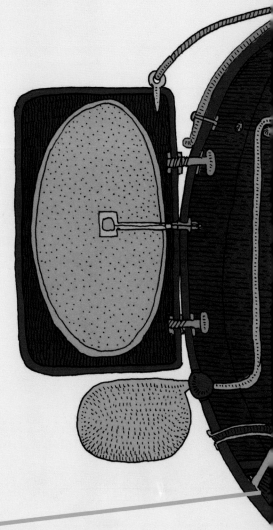

Pump

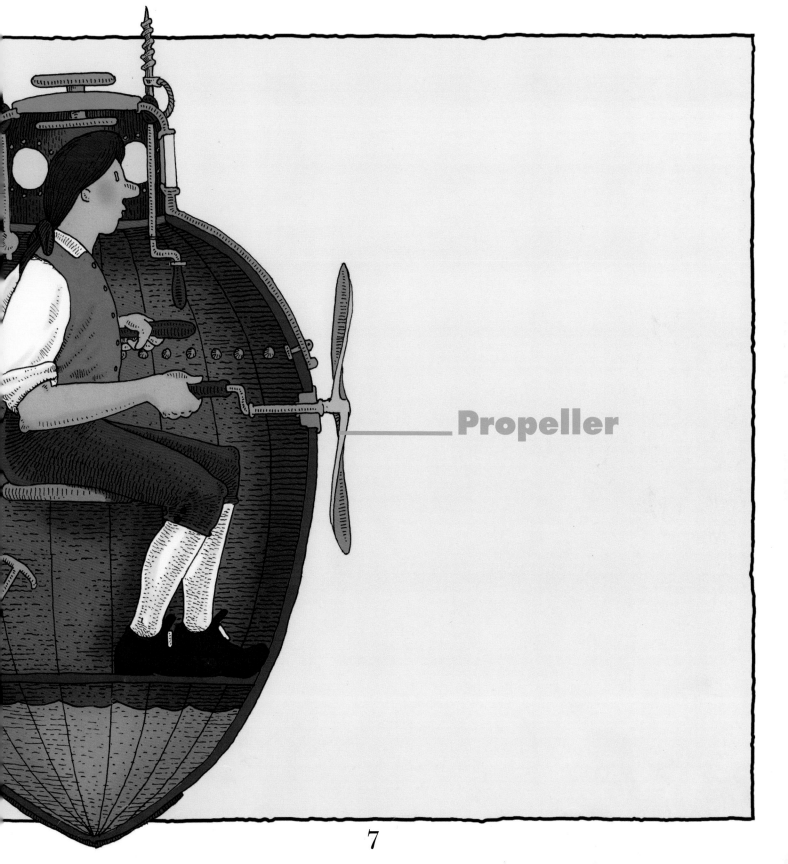

_____ **Propeller**

U-boats were
German subs. They
would sink enemy ships.

U-Boat U 81

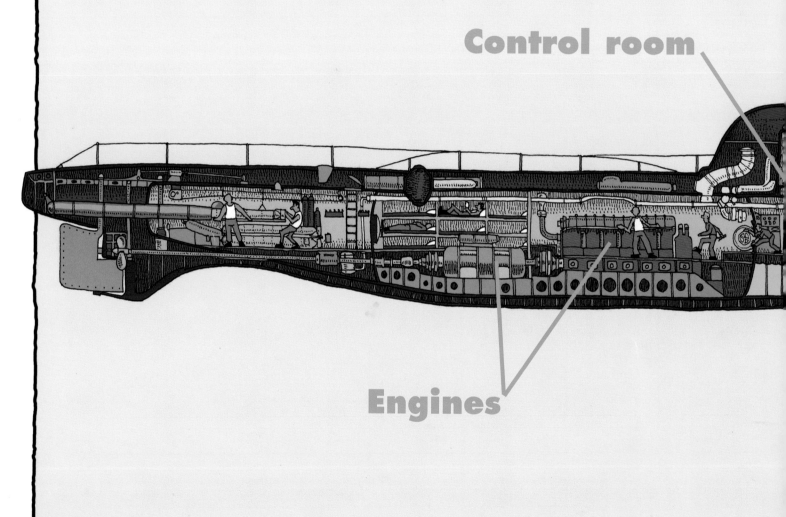

Control room

Engines

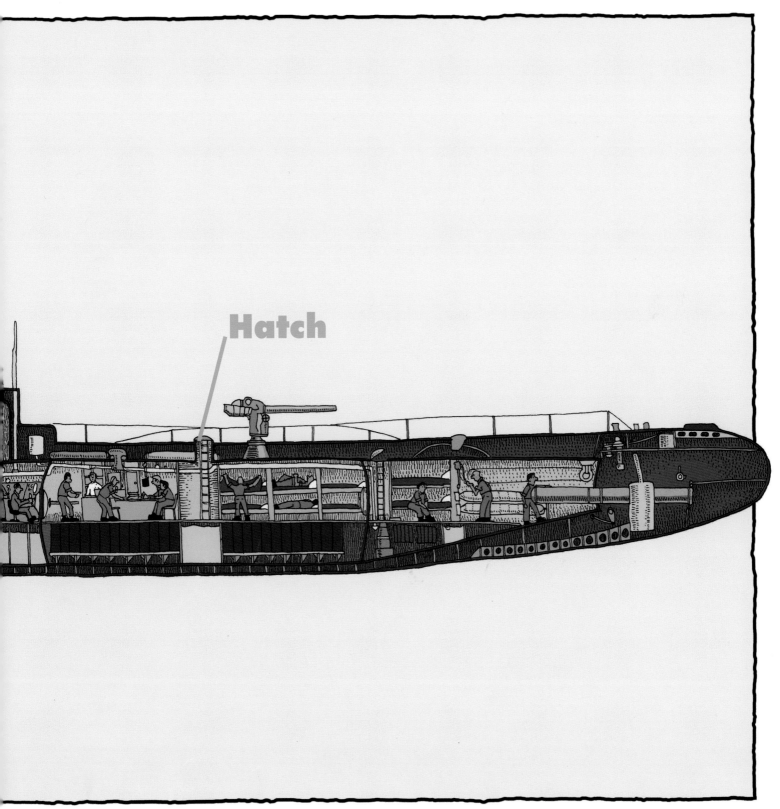

Hatch

Midget Submarines

Midget subs were used in wars, too. They attacked big ships.

X-Class Submarine

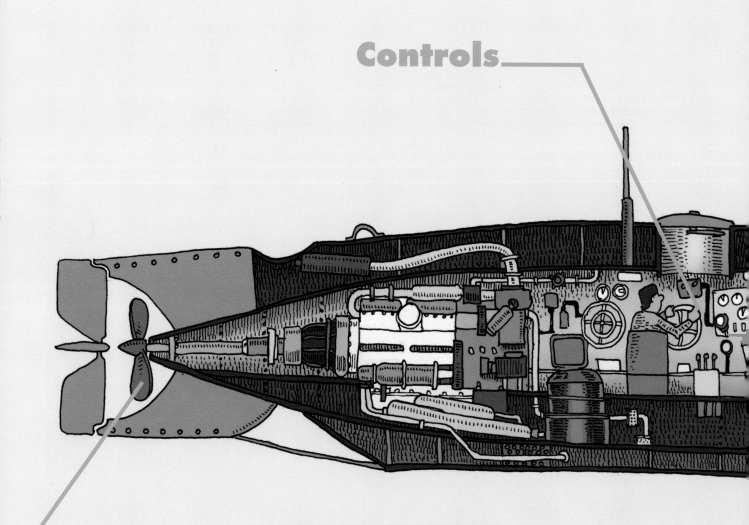

Controls

Propeller

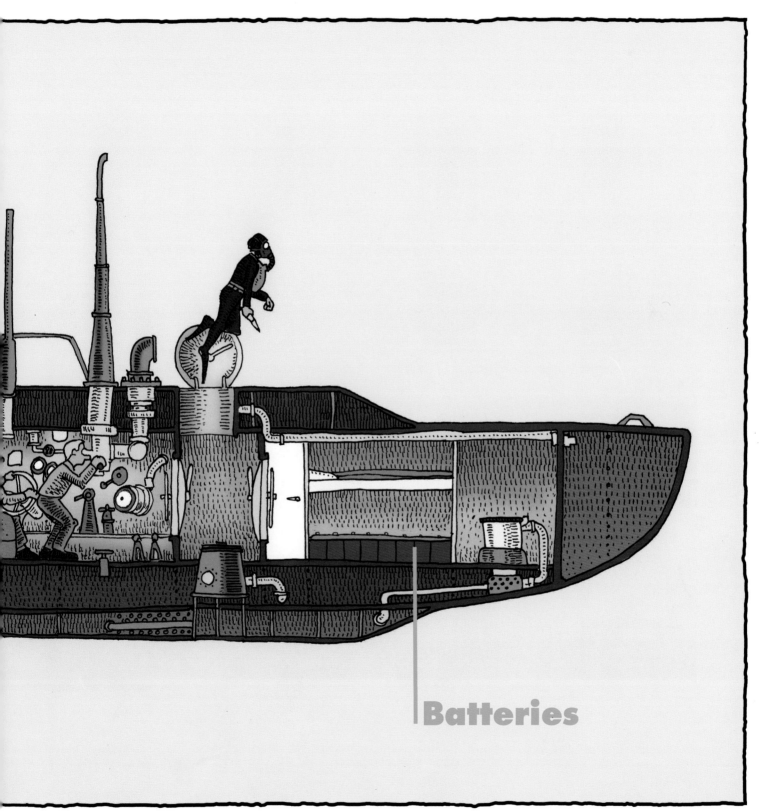

Batteries

Modern Submarines

Today, subs use nuclear power.
They stay underwater for months.

Nuclear Submarine

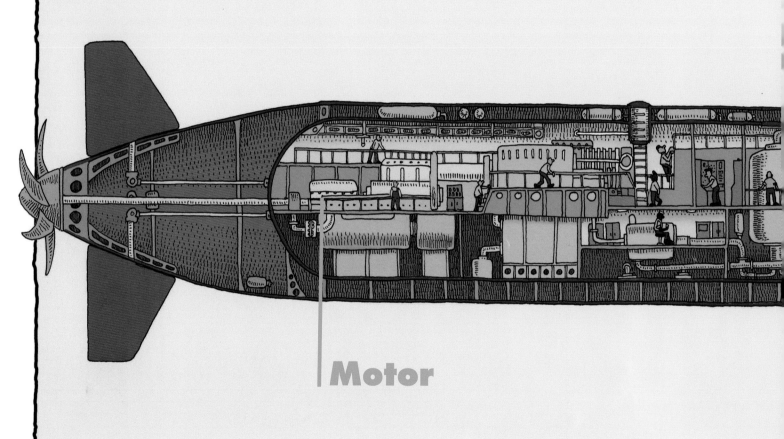

Motor

18

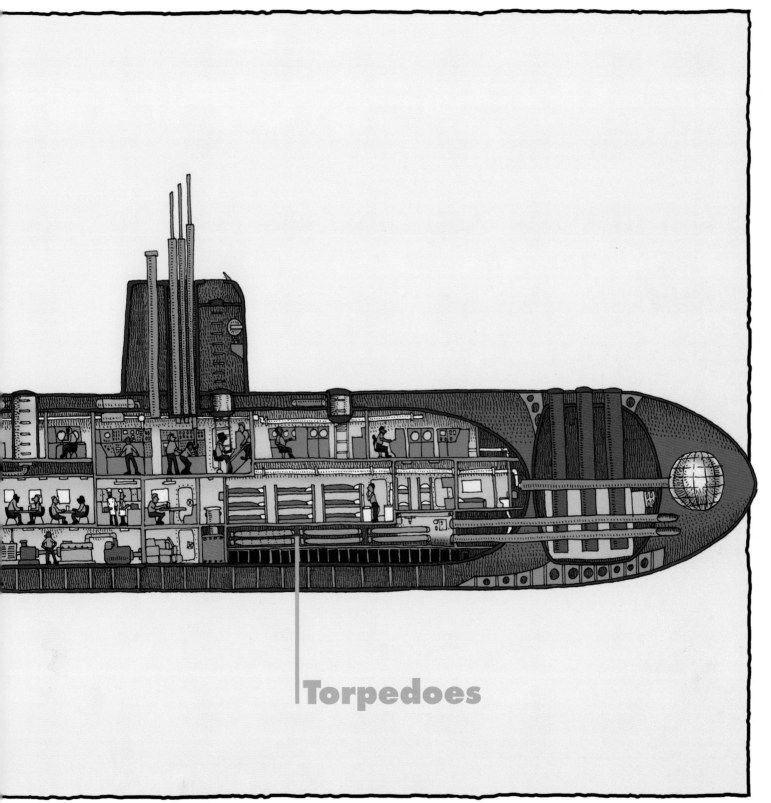

Torpedoes

Submersibles

Small subs explore the oceans. They can go deeper than large subs.

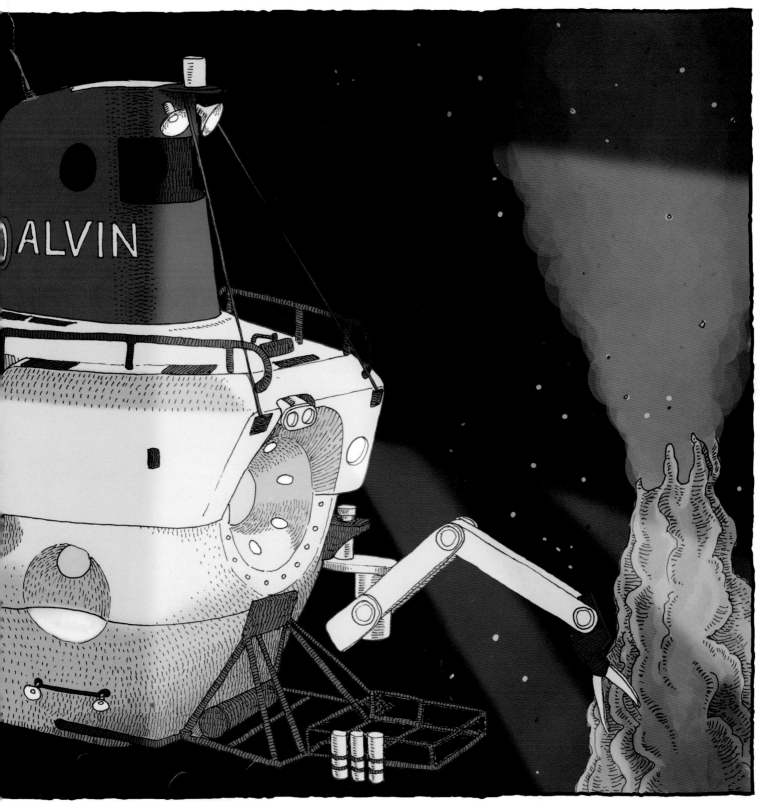

DSV Alvin

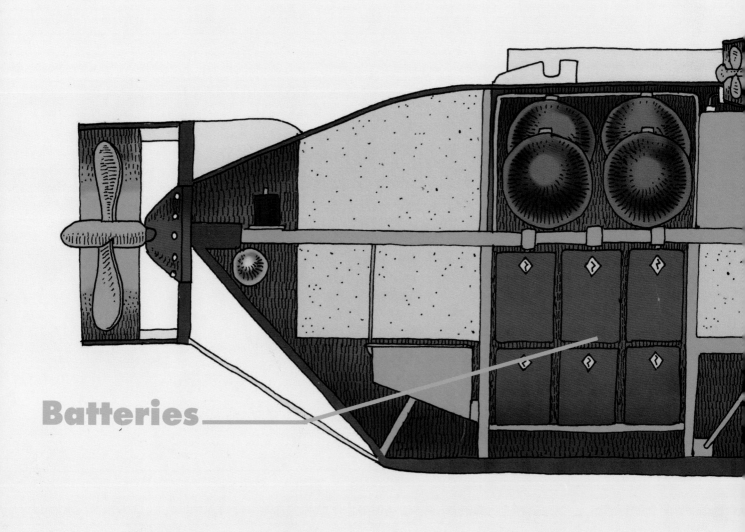

Batteries

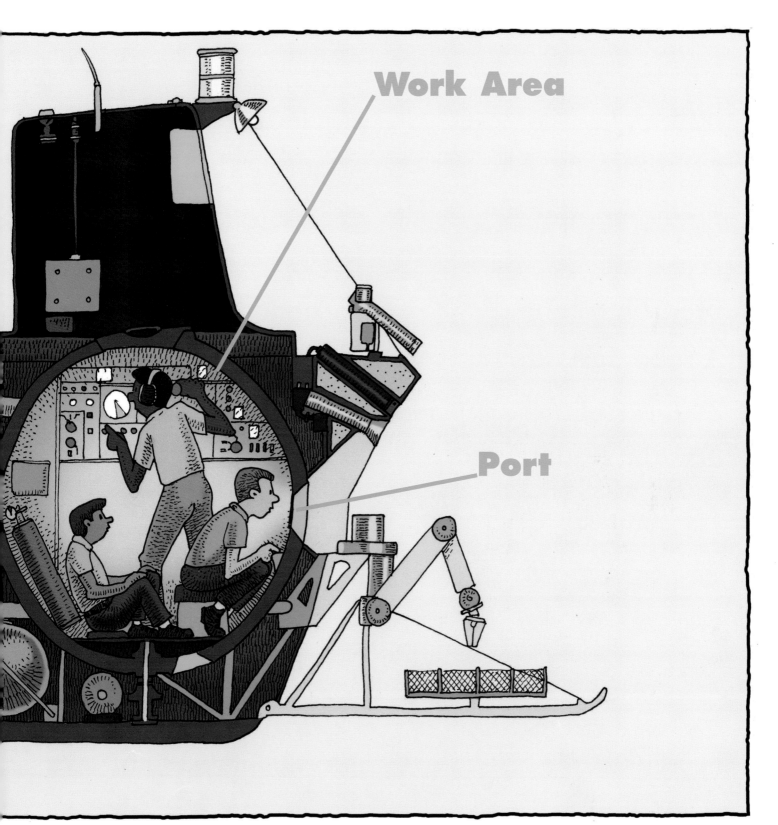

Work Area

Port

Glossary

battery

Electric cells that provide power

breathing tube

A tube that allows people to receive air to breathe under water

nuclear reactor

A device that uses atomic power to produce energy

torpedo

A self-contained underwater weapon

Index